MW01167012

Secret Scars

WHAT YOU NEED TO KNOW ABOUT CUTTING

by Terry O'Neill

Content Adviser:
Billy AraJeJe Woods, Ph.D.,
Department of Psychology, Saddleback College,
Mission Viejo, California

Reading Adviser:
Alexa L. Sandmann, Ed.D.,
Professor of Literacy, College and Graduate School
of Education, Health, and Human Services,
Kent State University

Compass Point Books
151 Good Counsel Drive
P.O. Box 669
Mankato, MN 56002-0669

Copyright © 2010 by Compass Point Books
All rights reserved. No part of this book may be reproduced without written
permission from the publisher. The publisher takes no responsibility for the use of
any of the materials or methods described in this book, nor for the products thereof.
Printed in the United States of America.

 This book was manufactured with paper containing
at least 10 percent post-consumer waste.

Photographs ©: Capstone Press/Karon Dubke, cover, 10, 14, 33, 36 (right);
Shutterstock/Peter Weber, 5; Shutterstock/Anita Patterson Peppers, 7;
Getty Images Inc./Peter Dazeley/Photographer's Choice, 8; iStockphoto/
Blue_Cutler, 15; Getty Images Inc./altrendo images, 16; Shutterstock/Diego
Cervo, 17; iStockphoto/katsgraphicslv, 20; iStockphoto/pink_cotton_candy,
22; iStockphoto/quavondo, 25; Shutterstock/Yuri Arcurs, 27; iStockphoto/
digitalskillet, 28; iStockphoto/Bryngelzon, 29; iStockphoto/killerb10, 30; 123RF/
mccale, 35; iStockphoto/cglade, 36 (left); iStockphoto/barsik, 37; Newscom,
38; iStockphoto/JeanellNorvell, 39; Getty Images Inc./Kevin Cooley/Stone, 41;
iStockphoto/aldomurillo, 42.

Editor: Brenda Haugen
Page Production: Heidi Thompson
Photo Researcher: Marcie Spence
Art Director: LuAnn Ascheman-Adams
Creative Director: Joe Ewest
Editorial Director: Nick Healy
Managing Editor: Catherine Neitge

Library of Congress Cataloging-in-Publication Data
O'Neill, Terry, 1944–
   Secret scars : what you need to know about cutting / by Terry O'Neill;
   content adviser, Billy AraJeJe Woods ; reading adviser, Alexa L. Sandmann.
      p. cm.—(What's the issue?)
   Includes index.
   ISBN 978-0-7565-4142-2 (library binding)
   1. Cutting (Self-mutilation) 2. Self-mutilation in adolescence.
   3. Adolescent psychology. I. Title. II. Series.
   RJ506.S44O54 2010
   616.85'8200835—dc22   2009006921

Visit Compass Point Books on the Internet at *www.compasspointbooks.com*
or e-mail your request to *custserv@compasspointbooks.com*

TABLE OF CONTENTS

CHAPTER one

WHO CUTS?

High school was not a happy time in Lori's* life. She's a college student now, and she feels in control of her life. But in high school she had problems with her parents, she had problems growing up in a small town, and she had problems with school cliques. Nothing seemed to work the way she wanted. That's when she got started as a cutter.

"One day I got the urge to hurt myself and started cutting," Lori said. "My parents never really knew about the cutting until much later, but my mom knew something was wrong. She would ask me if I needed help, if I wanted to talk to someone. I knew she was trying to be sympathetic, but it just irritated me. You know how when you're depressed, you sometimes don't want anyone to help? You say you don't need help. And it's embarrassing—you have to admit you have a problem."

* This and other names in this book have been changed for privacy reasons, except when reported in the media.

Then one night in her junior year, Lori tried to commit suicide. She drove her car off the road into a deep ditch. That night changed her life.

"My parents took me to the emergency room. Then I had to stay at the hospital for two weeks in the psych ward," she says.

That stay changed Lori's outlook. She realized cutting was *causing* problems for her, not solving them. After she was released from the hospital, Lori started seeing a therapist on a regular basis. Lori was ready to make a change, and therapy taught her more healthy ways to deal with her negative feelings.

Hurting Bad

Only a few years ago, people didn't talk much about cutting. Most people hadn't even heard of it. Now we know more about it. We know that cutters hurt really bad inside and have a hard time dealing with that.

A cutter is someone who deliberately hurts himself or

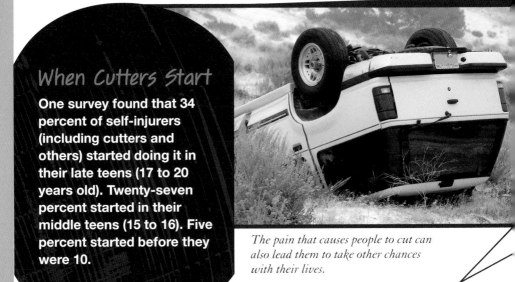

When Cutters Start

One survey found that 34 percent of self-injurers (including cutters and others) started doing it in their late teens (17 to 20 years old). Twenty-seven percent started in their middle teens (15 to 16). Five percent started before they were 10.

The pain that causes people to cut can also lead them to take other chances with their lives.

5

Great-Great-Grandma Was a Cutter, Too

Cutting isn't new. Accounts of self-injury go back to ancient times. The Greek historian Herodotus wrote in the fifth century B.C. about a Spartan leader who mutilated himself with a knife—severely and on purpose. References to self-injury—what we would call cutting—can also be found in the Bible. In Leviticus and Deuteronomy, for instance, Jehovah commands the people of Israel not to cut their bodies ritually as do the pagan nations around them.

Medical reports from past centuries show that cutting has continued through time. One example is Helen Miller. In 1875 Dr. Walter Channing discovered that the 30-year-old New York woman was slashing her arms and wrists. Channing also found pieces of glass, wooden splinters, needles, pins, shoe nails, and a piece of tin embedded in Miller's body. Channing reported that Miller sometimes cut her arms almost to the bone, yet she felt no pain when she cut.

herself by poking or slashing his or her skin with a sharp object. Some even carve words into their skin. Some cutters always use a favorite tool. It might be a razor, a pocketknife, a needle, or another sharp tool.

Cutters tend to hide their actions, so no one knows exactly how many people cut. It seems as if it's becoming more common. In part that's because the subject is more public than it

used to be. Today TV shows, books, and movies have characters who are cutters.

There's also a lot more information available in books and on the Internet. Not all of the Web information is good, but the fact that people can talk about cutting more openly is good. Some cutters feel less alone because they know they're not the only one.

Many teens turn to cutting to mask some other pain in their lives.

Too Many Cutters

Maybe you're a cutter. Or maybe you know someone who is. That wouldn't be surprising. Some researchers think that nearly 5 percent of people cut themselves on purpose at some time in their lives. One estimate is that 2 million to 3 million Americans are cutters. Some cut themselves often, year after year. One study found that kids self-mutilated, or hurt themselves, from once to 745 times a year.

Lori says: "I would use anything I had around me, but I usually carried a box cutter in

> "I would use anything I had around me, but I usually carried a box cutter in my purse. That way I could cut whenever I felt the need."

my purse. That way I could cut whenever I felt the need. One of my friends used dull-edged scissors. One day she had a really big gouge on her leg from using those scissors."

7

17 Percent

Cornell University professors Janis L. Whitlock and John J. Eckenrode wanted to know how common self-injury is among students. They surveyed 3,069 students at two universities. Seventeen percent said they had purposely cut or burned themselves, and almost 75 percent of those had done it many times.

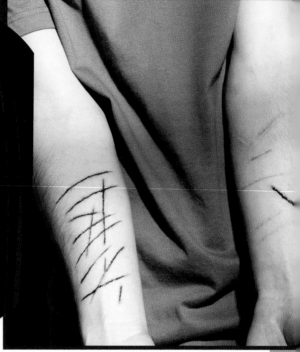

Cutting can leave permanent scars and even lead to dangerous infections.

Some cutters don't care what they use as long as it's sharp. Alison Mason, a school guidance counselor, says an art teacher sent a girl to her office one day. "Alysha came in, and I asked her to pull up her sleeve. She had long marks all the way up her arm, about a half-inch apart," Mason said. "She had used razor blades from the art department to do this."

Some teen cutters barely scratch themselves, but others cut deep, drawing blood and leaving permanent scars. Some cut only a few times, but some keep cutting themselves for many years.

Why Cutting?

Anyone can be a cutter. Lori was popular and on the dance team. She got good grades and has a nice family that does lots of things together. From the outside, she seemed to have an ideal life. On the inside, she was angry and hurting.

Lori started cutting when she was 15. A few cutters start as early as 6 or 7 years old, but most start during their teen years. Some stop after only a few months or years, but many keep cutting themselves through their 20s or even longer.

Doctors call cutting self-injuring or self-mutilating behavior. Self-injury includes a wide range of things, from fingernail biting and scab picking to extreme self-harm, such as breaking bones, cutting off an arm or a leg, or gouging an eye. "Sometimes they do things like 'erasing,'" says Mason. "They use a pencil eraser and rub and rub until they've actually worn away the skin and caused it to bleed. Sometimes they make a specific shape, like a tattoo or a person's name. It's mostly girls, but boys do this, too."

Some guys say it's hard to be open about their cutting prob-

Who Cuts?

- Up to four times as many girls as boys are cutters. Boys are more likely to do other types of self-injuring behavior, such as punching themselves, running into walls and other objects, and picking fights. Cutters are more likely than other teens to be bisexual or question their sexuality.

- A lot of cutters are sensitive perfectionists who are disappointed, angry, and frustrated when things don't go perfectly.

- Up to half of cutters were sexually or otherwise abused.

- Cutters have a difficult time coping with strong feelings and speaking about their feelings.

lem because the media mostly portray it as a girl thing. A guy who goes by the name of Wedge says he started cutting just before

9

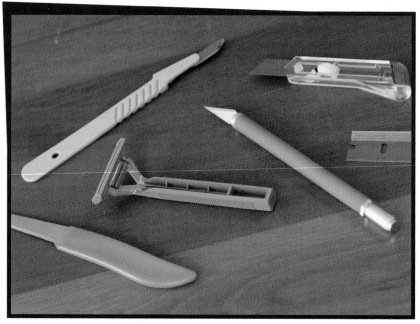

Some teens have a favorite tool they use when cutting, but many will just grab whatever is handy.

he hit his teens and then kept on going. "I turned to self-injury to deal with my distress, to make the pain 'real' and to ground myself, to just cope and get on with things," he said.

Adrian started cutting to make himself feel *something*—*anything* besides emptiness. Using razors, knives, and screwdrivers, Adrian made cuts on his legs and thighs. A lot of mornings he'd wake up with his pajamas stuck to the cuts. Then he'd pull the pajamas away from his legs so he could see the blood flow again. "I can't get over how much I enjoyed it," says Adrian. "I loved waking up in the morning and seeing that I had done something to myself."

Most cutters fall into one of two categories:

• Occasional cutters. They may cut when they feel certain kinds of stress, but they don't feel the need to do it all the time.

• Frequent cutters. They cut

frequently, and when they're not doing it, they're often thinking about doing it. Then something triggers their need, and they snap. They impulsively grab the nearest tool—or their special tool—and start cutting.

Keeping Secrets

You might not even know whether one of your friends is a cutter. A few teens do it to get attention from classmates and family members, but most cutters try to keep their habit a secret. "We pretty much kept our cutting a secret except from other kids we knew who did it, too," says Lori. "We could talk about it and not feel alone. Nobody else understood. With other people, if they knew, then they started asking lots of questions and talked about you. It was negative attention that you didn't want."

If someone happens to see their scars, cutters make up

What Do Self-Injurers Do?

52% Scratch or pinch themselves with finger-nails to cause bleeding or noticeable marks

38% Bang or punch objects (such as walls, rocks, and other hard surfaces) to cause bruis-ing or bleeding

34% Cut themselves

25% Punch themselves to cause bruising or bleeding

excuses like, "I was chasing my dog through some bushes," or "I fell and scraped my arm on the stair step."

Rituals

Many cutters make cutting into a ritual. They always cut in their bedroom, a certain bathroom, or a secret place outdoors. They

11

may play special music, burn candles, or do something else to set the mood. They use the same tool and often cut in the same place on their body over and over until the skin is too damaged to cut there anymore.

Even though they cut themselves on purpose, many cutters find that cleaning up afterward is just as important to them. Vanessa Vega is a woman who cut herself from her late teens into her early 20s. She wrote a book about her experiences. In it she tells what she did after cutting.

She first cleaned up the bathroom where she cut herself. She got rid of all the bloody tissues and towels and washed out the sink. Her cuts didn't hurt right away, but when the pain started, she would start to make herself feel better. She writes: "I clean my wounds, gingerly, carefully, lovingly. If there is a loose piece of skin, I tear it away. It sounds weird, but I want the wounds to look nice. I don't want them to appear jagged and random." Then, she says, she would take a shower and afterward, she would continue taking care of her wounds: "I find the bandages that will cover them the most and open them. I take out the antibiotic cream and apply it, with a swab, to my cuts. Then I put the bandages on and I wrap myself in my own arms."

Like many cutters, Vanessa found cutting comforting and even relaxing.

CHAPTER two

HIDDEN FEELINGS

If you're not a cutter, you probably find it hard to imagine why cutters would do this to themselves. Cutters have many reasons. For most, cutting helps them stop feeling so bad. They often feel as if their bad feelings were running out with the blood.

Lori says: "I would just get so upset and want some relief, so I would take out my box cutter and cut. Then I would feel better for a while."

Kids in Pain

For many cutters, something that happened when they were little kids leads them to cutting. Doctors know that a huge number of cutters were abused or neglected when they were young.

There are all kinds of abuse. Many cutters were sexually abused. Some cutters were beaten or punished in other harsh ways when they were little. Most of the time, these things happened to the children again and again.

In some cases, the cutter was neglected because the parents had drug problems or mental illnesses. Alison Mason says this was true of Alysha: "Her mother has a lot of problems and has been in and out of psych hospitals. She wanted to do the right thing, but because of her own problems, she had to leave the girl mostly with her grandfather. The mother couldn't even cope with her own life, much less the needs of her daughter."

Many cutters cut in the bathroom so they can easily clean up afterward.

Is Biology at Work, Too?

For some people, cutting eleases endorphins in the brain. These brain chemicals reduce tension and emotional distress and may lead to a feeling of calm. Researchers at the University of Washington, Seattle, have also found that girls who cut themselves have lower-than-average levels of serotonin. A low level of this mood-regulating brain chemical makes it harder to control emotions, so the impulse to cut is harder to resist.

Abused or neglected kids may become cutters as a way to deal with their suffering.

Sometimes the cutter's parents lost a job or a partner, or had an illness, such as cancer. This caused so much stress for the parents that they weren't able to think about their kids' needs even though the kids were worrying and suffering, too.

Experts say that in situations like this, a child comes to believe negative things about himself or herself that are not true, such as:

- I'm a bad person who deserves to be punished.
- There's something wrong with me that makes me unlovable.

Young people create their own rules, in order to cope with a situation:

- I'm safer if I'm "invisible"—if I don't draw attention to myself.
- If I speak up, I'll be hurt.

Young people may also come to conclusions that are all too true:

- I'm too weak to control what happens to me.
- I can't count on my parents to take care of me.

15

You Don't Count

Some kids are discouraged from expressing anger by their parents, so the kids learn how to hide their feelings instead of dealing with them. There's an old saying: "Children should be seen and not heard." This is how it is in some families. Parents don't want their kids to talk back or complain. When kids cry or show their angry feelings, they get yelled at or punished. This kind of treatment makes kids believe that no one cares about their feelings and that their feelings don't count. Instead of feeling loved and secure, they feel invisible, ignored, and unimportant. A few kids who feel like this turn to cutting.

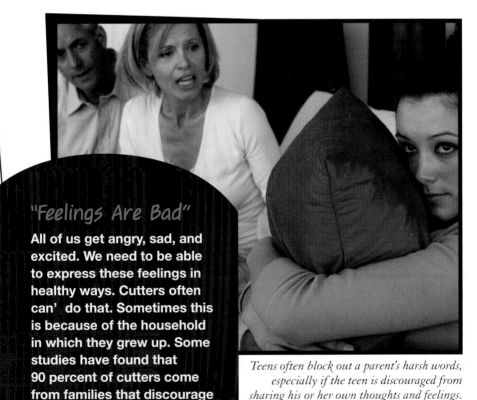

"Feelings Are Bad"

All of us get angry, sad, and excited. We need to be able to express these feelings in healthy ways. Cutters often can' do that. Sometimes this is because of the household in which they grew up. Some studies have found that 90 percent of cutters come from families that discourage the expression of feelings.

Teens often block out a parent's harsh words, especially if the teen is discouraged from sharing his or her own thoughts and feelings.

I'm in Control

Sara explains why she cuts: "It's like the whole world is telling you you're nothing, that you don't matter. Like you don't have a right to your feelings; you hear that enough and you start to believe it. When I cut, I'm in control of how many cuts I make, how big they are, what shape, how deep."

Sexual Confusion

Some teen cutters suffer from sexual confusion. They don't understand their own sexuality. Maybe they aren't sure whether they're straight or gay. Or maybe they think their sexual orientation wouldn't be accepted by the people they know. This can make them feel as if they have to hide their true selves, as if it's bad or something to be ashamed of. The stress of having a secret life can lead them to cut.

Why Cut Now?

Cutters usually cut themselves when they're feeling a lot of stress. They might feel the need to cut after a huge fight with a parent or friend, when someone bullies them, or when they feel overwhelming anger or depression. We all feel upset because of things like this, but for cutters, the stress builds up until they can't stand it anymore. They have to find a way to relieve the stress. For cutters, the relief comes when they hurt themselves. The pain of cutting the skin somehow stops the pain of feeling sad or angry.

There are other things that can

It's OK to feel upset about a bad test or a fight with a friend, but for cutters, this stress leads them to do unhealthy things.

cause a cutter to pick up a knife, too. These are called triggers. Seeing someone else's scars, or a photo of them, can trigger some cutters' need to cut. Hearing a certain song, being with a friend who cuts, or reading about another cutter's experiences may also be a trigger.

Triggers work because for many cutters, cutting is an impulsive act. They don't carefully plan their next cutting session. When something sets them off, they feel as if they just have to do it.

Is Cutting Suicidal?

Studies have found that teens who have more than one cutting episode are six times as likely as other teens to have thought about or attempted suicide. Yet most experts agree that the cutting itself isn't usually suicidal. When feeling terrible pain and despair that would drive some people toward suicide, a cutter slashes his or her skin instead.

Some doctors view cutting as

Afraid of Happiness

Psychologists say it isn't only painful emotions that cutters can't handle well. Many cutters have had such unhappiness in their lives that they're afraid to be happy. They don't think they deserve it. So if they start to feel happy, they get scared and cut themselves to get back to their normal state of mind.

a short-term way of coping with uncontrollable feelings. They believe that with good care, people who practice this dangerous form of "self-help" can learn more healthy ways to survive their pain.

Still, cutting is dangerous, even if you don't want to commit suicide. Cutters are usually careful not to harm themselves seriously, but the knife can slip and cut too deep. Or the wounds can become badly infected even if the cutter takes care of them. Cutting is one way to cope with bad feelings, but it's not a healthy way.

CHAPTER three

MORE THAN CUTTING

Cutters often have other problems besides cutting. It's not uncommon for a cutter to have an eating disorder, too. Various experts say that 35 percent to 80 percent of cutters have other problems.

Cutters often have emotional problems such as depression or substance abuse.

Like many cutters, Lori started with one kind of problem—an eating disorder called bulimia—and added another—cutting. "I had some friends who were cutters, too," she says. "They and a lot of other kids, too, had eating disorders, and some were binge drinkers."

Two of the most common problems cutters share are eating disorders and dissociation.

Eating Disorders

You might know people with eating disorders. They might have anorexia. They diet all the time even though they're already skinny. Or maybe they are bulimic—eating meals and snacks but then forcing themselves to vomit it all up. It's not only skinny people who have eating disorders. People who are overweight usually have an eating disorder, too. People who weigh 100 pounds (45 kilograms) or more over what's healthy are probably compulsive overeaters —they can't stop themselves from overeating.

All of these eating disorders are extremely dangerous. They're part of a pattern of what doctors call self-destructive behavior—things people do to hurt themselves. Cutting is also part of this pattern.

Like cutters, people with eat-

Up to 7 percent of women suffer from bulimia at some time in their lives. This eating disorder usually starts in the teen years.

Like a Drug

Doctors say that cutting can become almost like a drug. Sara agrees. "[Cutting] becomes so much a part of your life, you find it's all you think about from the moment you wake up until you go to bed at night," she says. "Once you find that it works for you, it becomes your drug of choice. It's easy to justify because you aren't hurting anyone but yourself. It's not illegal like pot and other drugs, so you tell yourself it's OK."

ing disorders often make rituals for themselves, try to keep their habits secret, and feel shame about their secret.

Those who cut, undereat, or overeat do so to release tension, get rid of feelings of anger, sadness, or other strong emotions, or distract themselves from feeling bad about themselves.

Both cutters and people with eating disorders are trying to take control of their out-of-control emotional lives. By cutting or eating a whole gallon of ice cream or refusing to eat anything at all, two things happen: They get a temporary emotional high, and they feel

as if they're in control because they've *chosen* the harmful behavior instead of doing what someone else would want them to do (not cut, eat sensibly). These two "benefits" make it difficult to give up the harmful behavior. The bottom line is that people use both types of behavior to try to gain control over some aspect of their lives that otherwise seems uncontrollable.

Out of Body, Out of Mind

Do you ever daydream? Maybe you're in English class, but your mind is on your boyfriend or girlfriend or what you're going

21

to do after class. You're not even aware of your surroundings or the passing time. Then the teacher asks you a question, and suddenly you're back in reality. Dissociation is like that, only to an extreme.

Many cutters experience dissociation when they cut. Some don't feel any pain when they cut. It's only later, when they're back in reality, that they feel the pain. Some feel as if they were outside their body watching themselves cut. Vanessa, a longtime cutter, writes that she often went into a trance when she cut. Here's what she says about one experience: "Time stands still. I don't know how long I've been cutting. Part of me can see my arm, but there isn't any pain, and so I don't know if it's real."

"Part of me can see my arm, but there isn't any pain, and so I don't know if it's real."

Just about everybody daydreams once in a while, but cutters often feel disconnected from their bodies.

Are Tattoos, Piercing, and Cutting Related?

Years ago people with tattoos, piercings, and other forms of body art were considered outsiders. People viewed these markings as self-mutilation, like cutting. Yet many experts today point out that there are important differences. People with tattoos and piercings like to show them off, but most cutters hide their scars. Also, the person with tattoos or piercings decides that putting up with the pain to get these decorations is worth it. Cutters aren't trying to decorate themselves; instead, they seek out pain and blood, damaging themselves to get rid of other painful feelings. Further, a certain amount of time and pain are required when getting tattoos or piercings. For a cutter, the time and pain involved in cutting aren't limited.

When you daydream, you can quickly bring yourself back to reality. Cutters who dissociate can't always come back so easily. Some cutters dissociate so severely that they experience amnesia. They're shocked when they wake up and see blood and gashes on their skin. They might even find themselves someplace and not know how they got there.

Some cutters feel away from reality even when they're not cutting. They feel as if they're living life in a fog. They function automatically—they take part in conversations, school, work, and social events, but they don't really feel a part of these experiences. For these people, cutting breaks the spell. It brings them back to reality and connects them to the world once again.

CHAPTER four

MY FRIEND'S A CUTTER —WHAT CAN I DO?

It's scary to find out that a friend is deliberately cutting himself or herself. Maybe you found out by accident. Maybe your friend's shirtsleeve got pulled up and you saw a bunch of scabs or scars. Or maybe your friend told you the secret.

It's natural to feel afraid for your friend, and you might even feel afraid *of* your friend. You might be worried that you don't know what to do. There's no single right way to behave, but you can do some things to help.

Helping

You probably can't solve your friend's problems by yourself, but you can let your friend know you're there for support.

If your friend is a cutter, letting him or her know you care is often the best thing you can do.

Tell your friend that you're worried but that you want to help if you can. Many cutters say that this is the best thing you can do. After all, one reason teens cut is that they don't feel they have anyone they can count on. When a friend steps up and offers support, it can make a lot of difference.

If your friend is willing to talk about cutting, listen. Many cutters feel shame and embarrassment about their cutting and find it really hard to tell someone that they're doing it. So if you

Signs to Notice

If your friend has several of the behaviors listed below, you're right to be concerned:

- Has frequent mood swings
- Doesn't seem to like himself or herself
- Often acts on impulse rather than thinking things through
- Is often sad or tearful
- Is constantly angry
- Is anxious or nervous
- Can't seem to think of anything good about his or her life
- Wears long sleeves and long pants, even during hot weather
- Often has unexplained cuts, bruises, and scabs
- Avoids activities, such as swimming, that require undressing or showing skin

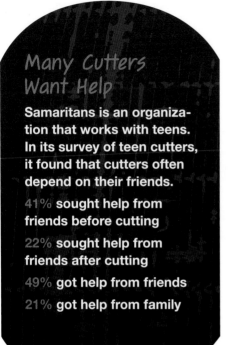

Many Cutters Want Help

Samaritans is an organization that works with teens. In its survey of teen cutters, it found that cutters often depend on their friends.

41% sought help from friends before cutting

22% sought help from friends after cutting

49% got help from friends

21% got help from family

says. "In our school, an outside agency comes in and works with the kids. But when a student who cuts comes to my office, I mostly listen to what they have to say. I don't ask them *why*. I just encourage them to say what they want to. I ask them if it hurts. A lot of the time, they say they don't even feel it."

Encourage your friend to seek help. Suggest talking to a trusted adult.

If your friend can't talk to his or her parents, maybe there's a teacher or school counselor your friend feels comfortable with. Offer to go along. Sometimes having a friend close by can make it easier.

Try to be available when your friend needs your support. You can talk on the phone, play a video game, or suggest some activity you can do together. If you're doing something together, your friend won't be cutting.

If you're worried, tell some-

can, encourage your friend to talk about what he or she is feeling and what problems may be causing the cutting. Sometimes having someone who will listen without making judgments can relieve some of the stress and pain.

School counselor Alison Mason says that's what she does when a cutter comes to her office. "I don't do treatment," she

Fun distractions are one way to help cutters refrain from hurting themselves.

one who can help. Your friend might not want you to tell anyone. He or she might even threaten to end your friendship if you do. You'll have to decide which is more important— getting help for your friend or keeping him or her from being angry with you.

What About Your Parents?

If your parents know that your friend is a cutter, they might want you to stop seeing him or her. Some parents are afraid that cutting is contagious. They might worry that if you have a friend who cuts, you'll do it, too. That might seem silly to you, but

If you or a friend is a cutter, talking to a trusted adult can sometimes help more than you think.

it does happen sometimes. For example, Lori says that when she was a cutter, "the more people heard about it, it seemed like the more people did it." Many experts agree. Mason says she's heard of kids cutting together, and she says one friend's cutting can lead another friend to try it, too.

If your parents are worried, the best thing you can do is be open and honest with them. Tell them why you're concerned about your friend and why you want to help. They might have some good ideas, and they might be willing to let your friend come to your house to visit even if they don't want you going someplace alone with him or her.

What Not to Do

Don't freak out. Freaking out will probably make your friend not trust you with any secrets again.

Don't try to force your friend to talk about the cutting, but make it clear that you're willing to listen when he or she is ready to talk.

Don't tell your friend that he or she is stupid or crazy, and don't gossip about your

Talking to your friend about cutting may be scary, but being calm and supportive can sometimes help.

29

Cutters often hide their scars by wearing long sleeves.

friend. These things don't help. They'll just make your friend feel worse.

Don't try to convince your friend that he or she has a wonderful life. Even with a beautiful home, good grades, nice clothes, and the latest cell phone, your friend is in pain. Trying to convince your friend that he or she has nothing to feel bad about can make your friend feel as if you don't believe his or her feelings are real.

Don't threaten to stop being friends if he or she won't stop cutting. Ultimatums don't work. If your friend is in deep emotional pain, he or she will probably choose cutting instead of your friendship.

Don't expect your friend to stop cutting quickly. The cutting may be caused by deep-seated problems. It can take years of trying for some people to get strong enough to stop cutting entirely.

Take Care of Yourself

Remember that you aren't responsible for your friend's behavior. If you're a good friend, you probably want to help. Know that there may come a time when the situation is too much for you. Even if your friend wants to depend on you, you might need to take a break from your friend and his or her problems. Don't feel guilty if this time comes. It's more important to take care of yourself than to keep trying to help your friend. You can't help your friend if you're drowning, too.

CHAPTER five

I THINK I NEED HELP

Are you ready to stop cutting? Maybe you started cutting almost by accident. One day when you were feeling sad or mad, you just took a razor blade and made a cut on your arm. You might have been surprised to find that it made you forget how bad you were feeling.

It might even have made you feel good, so you did it another time when you felt bad. Before you knew it, you were cutting more often. It became a habit.

The sad thing is that this habit is only a temporary fix for your bad feelings. When you cut, it's like popping a balloon, says Armando Favazzo, a psychiatrist who has worked with cutters for many years. All the pressure of built-up emotions is suddenly gone. However, Favazza adds, the stress only goes away for a few hours or a few days. Whenever you get stressed or anxious again, you have to cut again.

Not only that, but cutting adds its own stress because it makes you feel worried and ashamed. You know it's not a healthy thing to do. When you decide you want to quit, you're making an important decision. Quitting isn't easy, but you can do it. The first and most important step is wanting to stop.

Ways to Help Yourself

Some cutters can quit all by themselves, but many can't. If you want to stop, here are some things you can try.

Cutting is a dangerous short-term solution to problems. Doctors warn that cutting might only get worse without some form of help, and the underlying problems leading to the cutting won't magically go away.

- Make rules for yourself. Don't try to stop cutting all at once. That can be such a big job that you'll get discouraged and give up if you fail. So give yourself some rules. One teen made the rule that she couldn't cut when she was on her bed, which had been her favorite place to do it. Another got a timer. When she wanted to cut, she made herself wait a half hour. Sometimes by the time the timer went off, the urge wasn't as strong, and she could keep herself from cutting. As you get stronger and are able to follow one rule, you can set more limits.

- When you get the urge to cut, force yourself to stop and try to think clearly about what you're feeling. What happened that makes you want to cut right now? Is there a way to feel better besides cutting?

- When you get the urge to cut, remind yourself why you want to quit. Lori reminds herself of her stay in a psychiatric ward. "The hospital experience kicked me in the butt," she says. "Some of the people there were really out of control. And we had group

When You Tell a Friend

Choose a friend you trust, but keep in mind that your secret may be shocking to this person. At first your friend may be afraid of you or angry or disgusted with you. Give your friend time to think about what you say. Give him or her permission to ask you questions. If you're not ready to talk about something yet, tell your friend that. Let him or her know why you've chosen to share this secret.

stuff where we had to talk about ourselves. I just felt 'I don't belong here. I'm not like this. This is not me.'"

- Tell someone you trust. Choose a friend, parent, or other person you trust. Tell the person about your cutting and that you're try- ing to stop. Ask him or her to be a support person for you—some- one you can go to when you feel the urge to cut. Lori says, "You feel like no one will understand, but someone will."
- Keep yourself busy. When you feel the urge to cut, walk your dog, call a friend,

rake leaves, clean your room, or do something else that will distract you from cutting. Make a list of things you can

Getting some fresh air and playing catch with your dog can be a great option when you feel the urge to cut.

Instead of Cutting ...

Do something that has some of the same effects as cutting but won't harm you:

- Put a heavy rubber band on your arm and snap it hard several times until the urge to cut goes away.
- Squeeze a handful of ice until you feel the pain.
- Use a red marker to draw lines where you'd like to cut.

Express your feelings:
- Call or IM a friend and talk.
- Write about your feelings in a diary or journal.

Do something to distract you from the need to cut:
- Play a video game.
- Watch a funny movie.

Do something physical:
- Go for a bike ride.
- Go for a run, or shoot some hoops.
- Dance to some crazy music.

Do something calming:
- Take a bubble bath.
- Listen to soothing music.

Do something creative:
- Paint a picture, or play your guitar.
- Write a poem.

Do something for someone else:
- Do a chore for a neighbor.
- Clean up the kitchen for your mother.

You can try some of these ideas, or you can make your own list of things to do instead of cutting.

do instead of cutting. Pull out the list when you feel the urge.

- When you're ready, ask for help. Ask a parent or teacher to find a professional you can talk to, or contact one of the organizations listed on page 45. It may be a hard thing to do, but these people can help you stop.

- Don't give up. Most people can't give up a habit the first time they try. So don't be surprised or discouraged if it takes several attempts before you can quit cutting.

Friends can be a source of comfort and support during the quitting process.

Professional Help

Sometimes you can't quit cutting no matter how hard you try. You may need a therapist to help you stop cutting. A therapist is a type of counselor or doctor who works with people to help them solve their problems. Going to someone like that might sound scary, but therapists are caring

Some people can't get better without professional help. If you need help, talk to a parent or another trusted adult. They can help you find a professional who can help you gain the self-respect necessary to overcome your addiction to cutting.

people who want to help you take control of your life.

Your therapist will talk about your cutting with you. It may take several counseling sessions before your therapist is ready to recommend a treatment program. He or she might recommend individual counseling, group counseling with others who have problems similar to yours, family counseling, medication, hospital outpatient or inpatient treatment, or a combination of several of these.

Some treatment programs help you understand the root causes of your cutting and help you learn how to deal with these causes. The goal of treatment "is not to get rid of uncomfortable feelings but rather to understand them and work them through directly so that they don't come back to haunt you," says psychologist Wendy Lader, head of S.A.F.E. (Self Abuse

Group therapy shows cutters they are not alone.

Finally Ends) Alternatives, one of the best-known programs that helps cutters.

Other programs focus on changing your behavior or your feelings and your reactions to the things that trigger your need to cut. Therapy can teach you how to examine the beliefs and attitudes that cause you to feel bad and to cut. Therapy can help you find healthy ways to deal with these things.

Telling Your Parents

So what's going to happen when you tell your parents? You might not want to do that, but you're probably going to have to tell them at some point. Sometimes a teacher, clergy member, or school counselor can help. School counselor Alison Mason says that if a student is sent to her because of cutting, she must tell the parents. "We have to do that if a kid is harming themselves," she says. "I tell the parents right away. Then, often, the student talks to the parents while I'm with them. I always offer to help them—be with them when they tell their parents in person or on the phone.

"Some parents just say something like, 'OK, I'll talk to her when she gets home.' Other parents cry and cry."

Most parents aren't going to get mad. Most will be worried and upset and want to find a way to help. You'll probably have a big feeling of relief when you finally share your troubling secret.

Last Cut

Whether you get the help of a therapist or find your own way to stop cutting, it will take a lot of hard work—and it will be worth it. You'll have a new, happier life. Nicole reports: "What got me to stop was something my social worker said. She said, 'You will always have emotional scars; do

"What got me to stop was something my social worker said. She said, 'You will always have emotional scars; do you want physical ones as well?'"

you want physical ones as well?'" Sara says, "For me it was the night I made over 300 cuts on my body without realizing it. That scared me enough to ask for help."

Alex was a cutter for years.

If you can't talk to your parents about cutting, go to another trusted adult.

41

When Cutters Stop

40% stopped within one year of starting

80% stopped within five years

With the help of therapy, she was able to quit cutting. She says, "Self-harm has been an important part of my life for 11 years. I am now realizing I may have outgrown the behavior. When I try to cut myself, I experience an unacceptable level of pain, as if my body is screaming, 'No.' … Although I miss the drama of self-harm, … I know that my life is fuller than it has been for a long time."

It may be tough asking for help to quit cutting, but the rewards are worth it.

QUIZ

Pick the most accurate answer, then check the results to see whether you should be concerned about your friend.

1. You're in the school bathroom and notice that your friend has several scabby cuts on his or her arm. Your friend:

    A) takes out some ointment and says, "Yeah, my cat scratched me. I've got to put this ointment on so they don't get infected."

    B) quickly pulls a sleeve down and says, "They're no big deal. I don't know how I got them."

2. Your friend is really smart in school. When he or she gets a B, his or her reaction is:

    A) "Wow, I guess I have to study harder for next week's test."

    B) tearing up the paper and saying, "I'm so stupid!"

3. Your school is having a dance after the Friday night ball game. Your friend:

    A) doesn't want to go but ends up going and having a great time there.

    B) wants to stay home and sneak some beer from the fridge.

4. You're at a swimming party. Your friend:

    A) jumps into the water wearing a swimsuit or swim trunks.

    B) heads for the water wearing a long-sleeved black T-shirt.

5. Your friend's purse spills. She quickly gathers up the contents. Among her things you notice:

    A) five lipsticks.

    B) a box cutter.

Results

If you have mostly B answers, your friend might be in trouble. For some ideas about what you can do to help, see Chapter 4. The "Additional Resources" and "Where to Get Help" sections near the end of this book also can help.

GLOSSARY

coping   facing and dealing with a problem

dissociation   feeling of unreality or detachment from one's body and everyday life

impulsively   spontaneously, without thinking about the consequences

ritual   pattern followed each time something is done

self-injury   harming oneself, usually as a way of coping with problems

self-mutilation   injuring one's body deliberately

substance abuse   using alcohol, drugs, or other substances in an unhealthy way

therapist   counselor or doctor who provides treatment to help a person overcome his or her problems

trigger   something or someone that sets off a process; in the case of cutting, a trigger is something that creates a desire to cut

WHERE TO GET HELP

Many crisis hotlines are confidential and don't keep records of the caller's phone number. If you're worried about this, ask about it when you make your first call. Hotline hours of operation may vary.

In addition to these organizations, look in your local telephone book under "Crisis Hotlines" and "Mental Health," or talk to a trusted parent, counselor, teacher, doctor, or clergy.

National Treatment Center
Del Amo Hospital
23700 Camino del Sol
Torrance, CA 90595
310/530-1151
helpline: 800/533-5266
Del Amo is a private behavioral health hospital with a wide range of programs that are tailored to each person's needs. The Youth Services Program is designed for clients ages 6 to 17 who can benefit from a highly structured and supervised setting.

S.A.F.E Alternatives
Linden Oaks Hospital at Edward
801 S. Washington St.
Naperville, IL 60540
708-366-9066
hotline: 800/366-8288
This organization offers information, inpatient and partial-hospitalization treatment programs, and referrals to therapists in most states.

The Trevor Project
Administrative Offices
9056 Santa Monica Blvd., Suite 100
West Hollywood, CA 90069
310/271-8845
helpline: 866/488-7386
This national crisis and suicide-prevention helpline provides support for gay, lesbian, bisexual, transgender, and questioning youth. The helpline is a free and confidential service that offers hope and someone to talk to 24 hours a day. Trained counselors listen and understand without judgment.

SOURCE NOTES

Chapter 1
Page 4, line 13: Lori. Rochester, Minn. Personal interview. 2 Aug. 2008.
Page 5, column 1, line 6: Ibid.
Page 7, column 2, line 2: Ibid.
Page 8, column 1, line 6: Alison Mason. Kansas City, Mo. Personal interview. 28 July 2008.
Page 9, column 1, line 17: Ibid.
Page 10, column 1, line 2: "Male Self Injury Taken Seriously." LifeSIGNS. 2 April 2009. *www.selfharm.org/what/male.html*
Page 10, column 2, line 3: Sue Vorenbeerg. "An Ugly Slice of Life." *Albuquerque Tribune*. 6 Feb. 2006.
Page 11, column 1, line 15: Lori.
Page 12, column 2, line 2: Vanessa Vega. *Comes the Darkness Comes the Light*. New York: AMACOM, 2007, pp. 60-61.

Chapter 2
Page 13, line 10: Lori.
Page 14, column 2, line 1: Mason.
Page 17, sidebar, line 2: Wendy Brown. "Conversations With Cutters." *Today's Parent*. November 2006, p. 176.

Chapter 3
Page 19, line 14: Lori.
Page 21, sidebar, line 2: "Conversations With Cutters," p. 176.
Page 22, column 2, line 6: *Comes the Darkness Comes the Light*, p. 4.

Chapter 4
Page 26, column 1, line 11: Mason.
Page 29, column 1, line 3: Lori.

Chapter 5
Page 34, column 2, line 5: Lori.
Page 35, column 1, line 20: Ibid.
Page 39, column 1, line 21: Kathiann M. Kowalski. "The Unkindest Cut." *Current Health*. January 2008, p. 27.
Page 40, column 1, line 14: Mason.
Page 40, column 2, line 13: "Conversations With Cutters," p. 178.
Page 40, column 2, line 18: Ibid.
Page 42, column 1, line 3: Alex Williams. "This Life." *Community Care*. 7 July 2005, p. 20.

Fiction

Carlson, Melody. *Blade Silver: Color Me Scarred*. Colorado Springs, Colo.: TH1NK, 2005.

Hopkins, Ellen. *Impulse*. New York: Simon Pulse, 2007.

Madsen, C. J. *Angels Fall From Gasoline Rainbows: A Novel*. Lincoln, Neb.: iUniverse, Inc., 2004.

Stoehr, Shelley. *Crosses*. New York: Backinprint.Com, 2003.

Nonfiction

Cobain, Bev. *When Nothing Matters Anymore: A Survival Guide for Depressed Teens*. Minneapolis: Free Spirit Publishers, 2007.

Esherick, Joan. *The Silent Cry: A Teen's Guide to Escaping Self-Injury and Suicide*. Philadelphia: Mason Crest Publishers, 2005.

Winkler, Kathleen. *Cutting and Self-Mutilation: When Teens Injure Themselves*. Berkeley Heights, N.J.: Enslow Publishers, 2003.

Internet Sites

FactHound offers a safe, fun way to find Internet sites related to this book. All of the sites on FactHound have been researched by our staff.

Here's all you do:
   Visit *www.facthound.com*
FactHound will fetch the best sites for you!

INDEX

ABOUT THE AUTHOR

Terry O'Neill has written and edited dozens of books for teens on topics such as biomedical ethics, animal rights, gender issues, and historical and political issues. She has a master's degree in American Studies from the University of Minnesota and is a former high school teacher.

ABOUT THE CONTENT ADVISER

Billy AraJeJe Woods has a doctorate in psychology, a master's degree in education, and a bachelor's degree in psychology. He has been counseling individuals and families for more than 25 years. He is a certified transactional analysis counselor and a drug and alcohol abuse counselor. A professor of psychology at Saddleback College, Mission Viejo, California, Woods teaches potential counselors to work with dysfunctional families and special populations. He began his counseling career in the military, where he worked with men and women suffering from post-traumatic stress disorder. In his practice, Woods has worked with many young adults.